The White House

Author: Karen Price Hossell

WORLD ALMANAC® LIBRARY

Please visit our web site at: www.worldalmanaclibrary.com
For a free color catalog describing World Almanac® Library's list
of high-quality books and multimedia programs, call 1-800-848-2928 (USA)
or 1-800-387-3178 (Canada). World Almanac® Library's fax: (414) 332-3567.

Library of Congress Cataloging-in-Publication Data

Price Hossel, Karen, 1957-
    The White House / by Karen Price Hossell.
       p. cm. — (Places in history)
    Includes index.
    ISBN 0-8368-5814-X (lib. bdg.)
    ISBN 0-8368-5821-2 (softcover)
    1. White House (Washington, D.C.)—Juvenile literature. 2. Washington (D.C.)—
Buildings, structures, etc.—Juvenile literature. I. Title. II. Series.
F204.W5P75   2005
975.3—dc22   2004061502

First published in 2005 by
World Almanac® Library
330 West Olive Street, Suite 100
Milwaukee, WI 53212 USA

This U.S. edition copyright © 2005 by World Almanac® Library. Original edition copyright © 2004
ticktock Entertainment Ltd. First published in Great Britain in 2004 by ticktock Media Ltd.,
Unit 2, Orchard Business Centre, North Farm Road, Tunbridge Wells, Kent, TN2 3XF.

Consultant: Adam Smith

Photo credits: AA World Travel Library: Alamy: 4–5; Associated Press Ltd: 13, 14L, 16L, 16R, 20BL, 21R, 22TL, 36–37,
Art Archive: 4B, 10, 26, 28L, 38L, Bridgeman Art Library: 4T, 6L, 8–9, 11L, Corbis: 5R, 11R, 12T, 12B, 14R, 15, 17, 20R,
21BL, 22BL, 23TR, 23B, 24TR, 24BL, 24BR, 25R, 27BR, 29L, 29R, 30B, 30T, 31, 32L, 32–33, 34L, 34–35, 35R, 36L, 37B,
38R, 39, 40, 41BL, 41TR, 44–45; Getty Images: 18–19; Library of Congress: 6–7, 7R, 18L, 19T, 27TL; Robin Kent: 9R,
Truman Library: 42

Printed in the United States of America

1 2 3 4 5 6 7 8 9 09 08 07 06 05

Contents

Introduction

A lthough it is only just over two hundred years old—young compared to some historical buildings around the world—the White House is rich in history. More than forty United States presidents and their families have lived there since November 1800, when John Adams and his wife became its first residents.

A New Capital

Before the White House was built, the official home of the president of the United States was, first, in New York City and, later, in Philadelphia. But early in U.S. history, government leaders decided they wanted their headquarters to

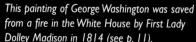

be more centrally located, so they purchased a strip of land where the borders of Virginia and Maryland met and began planning the new capital city. They decided to call the region the District of Columbia and later agreed also to call the city Washington, after President George Washington. One of the first buildings that should be erected, they agreed, was the president's home.

This painting of George Washington was saved from a fire in the White House by First Lady Dolley Madison in 1814 (see p. 11).

The government held a contest, inviting architects to submit plans for the new president's home. The winner was an Irish architect named James Hoban. The cornerstone was laid in 1792, and construction was completed in 1800. Along with Hoban, President Washington oversaw much of the mansion's construction. Washington, however, died in 1799, less than a year before it was finished.

Many Lives

Over its two-hundred-year history, hundreds of lives have been led inside the White House. Its rooms have resonated with the sounds of laughter and song, barking dogs and dancing feet. Children have slid down the banisters of the Grand Staircase and romped on the Great Lawn. Dignitaries from all over the world have attended dinners and concerts in the State Dining Room, as well as serious

The White House has been home to many children, including John F. Kennedy Jr., pictured here with his father.

meetings in the Cabinet Room. Brides and grooms have become wives and husbands in wedding ceremonies inside the White House and on its grounds. The silence of sorrow has filled the White House when family members and presidents themselves have died.

As the United States grew from a small, fledgling nation into the most powerful force in the modern world, the White House grew as well. Today, the White House is probably the most recognizable building in the United States. To most Americans, it symbolizes the strength and dignity of the United States presidency.

CHAPTER 1

How It Was Built

I n the late 18th century, the artist and engineer Pierre Charles L'Enfant worked with George Washington on the plans for a new capital city for the United States. L'Enfant thought the president's home should be built on a grand scale like a European palace. The Irish architect James Hoban won a competition to design the building. A workforce—consisting mainly of slaves— took eight years to build it.

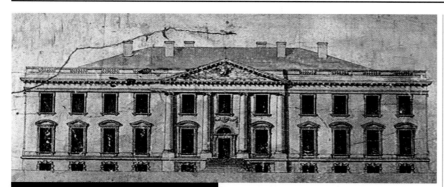

The winning design for the president's new home was drawn by Irish architect James Hoban.

A House Fit for a Leader

In 1790, the United States Congress, the lawmaking body of the United States, passed the Residency Act. This act provided for the establishment of a new city, to be called Washington. The city would be on a 6-square mile (16-square kilometer) piece of land on the shores of the Potomac River between the states of Virginia and Maryland. The precise location was personally selected by President Washington himself. The region the city was in was to be called the District of Columbia. Artist and engineer Pierre Charles L'Enfant worked with George Washington on the plans for the city. L'Enfant was born in France and was a major in the Continental Army during the American Revolution.

One of the first buildings to be constructed in Washington would be the home for the president. Congress determined that by 1800 the home should be ready to house the president and his family. In his design of the city, L'Enfant set aside 81.5 acres (33 hectares) for what he called the "President's Park." After the site was selected, leaders began to plan the buildings.

The Winning Architect

The secretary of state, Thomas Jefferson, announced a competition to design the new president's home. Nine architects submitted plans for the president's mansion, and James Hoban won the competition. Hoban was born in Ireland, and his design was based on a build-

This early drawing of the White House shows the crowd gathered for Andrew Jackson's inauguration in 1829.

Tales & Customs — Anglo-Palladian Style

The Anglo-Palladian architectural style is known for its square, geometric form. The front center of buildings designed in this style usually has a kind of porch, called a portico, with four columns and curved stairs on either side. The buildings are symmetrical, with matching windows on either side. Inside the front door of an Anglo-Palladian building would be a large entrance hall with a grand staircase.

ing in the city of Dublin, Ireland, called Leinster House. This grand house was built in the Anglo-Palladian style, which is based on the works of the 16th-century Italian architect, Andrea Palladio. English architects used many of Palladio's ideas in their designs. The president's mansion was also influenced by Georgian architecture, which is named after King George III, who was on the throne when the style became popular.

Once his plan was selected, Hoban moved to Washington, D.C., and began to oversee the construction of the president's mansion. He worked closely with President George Washington on the design. Hoban thought the president's house should have two stories and a raised base-

President George Washington oversaw the bulk of the building of the White House.

ment. The building would be constructed from sandstone. The cornerstone of the building was laid on October 13, 1792. Stonemasons were brought in from Scotland to carve the large blocks of sandstone used to construct the outside shell of the building. Few builders in America were used to working with sandstone, but Scottish stonemasons had perfected techniques of carving and laying the stone over hundreds of years.

The White House

This 18th-century engraving of stonemasons at work gives us an idea of the tools and methods that would have been used when building the White House. Stonemasons were recruited from Scotland, and the majority of the labor was carried out by slaves.

Solid as a Rock

President Washington had very specific ideas about how he wanted the president's house to look. In the 18th century, most homes were built out of wood. Some American leaders of the day thought the president's new home should be built from brick, but because it represented the strength and stability of the new nation, Washington thought the president's house should be built out of solid stone. The ornamental carvings around the windows and on other parts of the façade, Washington determined, should also be made of stone. The idea of stone carvings of rosettes and other decorations deviated from the usual Anglo-Palladian style, but Washington wanted to incorporate some of his own preferences into the design.

The Laborers

Besides stonemasons recruited from Scotland, other laborers—including slaves—worked on the

Tales & Customs — All in the Name

Until 1902, "White House" was not the official name of the home of the president of the United States; it was sometimes called the White House, but it was more often called the Executive Mansion. Its exterior walls were made from a grayish-brown sandstone, but when the building was whitewashed in 1798, the name "White House" became more commonly used. In 1901, President Theodore Roosevelt had the words "White House" printed on his stationery, making the name official.

home. Slavery had been in existence in the American colonies since about the middle of the 17th century, and Virginia and Maryland, the two states that had given up the sections of land that made up the District of Columbia, used a great deal of slave labor.

The White House's plaster façade features intricately designed details.

At first the commissioners of the District of Columbia planned to hire laborers from the United States and Europe, but few workers responded to their advertisements, so they soon decided to use slaves. African American slaves not only built most of the White House but they also worked on other government buildings in Washington, D.C., as well, including the Capitol.

From the beginning of construction in 1792 until November of 1800, the laborers worked every year during the milder months, from early spring to late autumn. The workers lived in shacks on the grounds, and the land around the president's new home was muddy and littered with trash from the workers and with leftover construction supplies. The building itself was constructed using a technique that had been

in use for thousands of years. The outer layer of stone that can be seen when one looks at the White House is backed by a layer of brick. This type of construction ensures that the White House is solidly built, which is one reason the building stands solid even after more than two hundred years.

Aquia Sandstone

The type of sandstone used to build the White House is called Aquia sandstone. It is a combination of quartz, pebbles, and clay pellets, held together by a sand hardened into stone. This sandstone came from a quarry along the Potomac River in Virginia. In 1791, L'Enfant was charged by Congress to find a source for the sandstone needed for the building. He purchased for the U.S. government the Wiggington's Island quarry, which is located alongside the Aquia Creek, in Virginia.

The stone used for the White House is called Aquia sandstone. It is the same material used for this column, which is part of the National Capitol Columns monument that stands in the National Arboretum in Washington, D.C.

*K*nown for many years as simply the "Executive Mansion," the White House has been a symbol of the United States presidency and government for more than two hundred years. While bearing witness to much political history, the White House has also endured two serious fires and various terrorist threats. All the while, the building has absorbed something of the personalities of its inhabitants through its many makeovers and renovations.

John Adams was the first U.S. president to live at the White House. When he first moved in, the mansion was far from finished.

First Residents

Because George Washington died in 1799, he never had a chance to see the completed building he helped to design. His successor, President John Adams,

and Adams's wife, Abigail, were the first residents at the White House. John Adams was one of the main leaders in the colonies' fight for independence, and his greatest presidential achievement was avoiding war with France through lengthy negotiations. This cool-headed, dignified way of diverting the war threat came during a time of public feeling that war was necessary. Adams, however, maintained that there was nothing to be gained through going to war.

The Adams family moved into the White House during November of 1800, even though it was not quite finished. When they first saw the building, they

may have been disappointed. There were almost no buildings in Washington, D.C., at the time and no landscaping or gardens around the mansion. The shacks used by the work crews still stood on the muddy, littered grounds. The plaster used to coat the walls of the house was still wet, and thirty-six of the rooms had not been plastered. The exterior walls of the building were a grayish-white. The house was not painted white for several years.

Advocate for Freedom

In 1801, former secretary of state Thomas Jefferson became president. Jefferson was a brilliant and inventive man who was a firm believer in the human

Time Line

1776	The colonies issue the Declaration of Independence.	
1783	Treaty of Paris is signed. Britain recognizes the United States following the American Revolution.	
1787	The U.S. Constitution is drafted and ratified by the individual states the following year.	
1789	George Washington becomes the first U.S. president.	

1790	A new capital city location is chosen and named Washington, D.C.	
1792	Thomas Jefferson announces competition to design new president's house. Irish architect, James Hoban wins.	
1800	President John Adams moves into the new residence, which is first known as the President's House or the Executive Mansion.	

The Declaration of Independence was drafted by Benjamin Franklin, John Adams, and Thomas Jefferson.

right to freedom. One of his greatest achievements was drafting the Declaration of Independence. Although highly intelligent, Jefferson was not comfortable with public speaking and often did his work behind the scenes.

A lover of architecture, when the contest for designs for the new president's house was announced, Jefferson anonymously submitted a design of his own. Jefferson made several changes to the White House, including redesigning the garden and planting hundreds of trees. He also built a wall around the house and oversaw construction of colonnades that led from the eastern and western sides of the house.

Lucky Save

The next residents were James Madison and his wife, Dolley. Dolley was popular with the public, and she was a great hostess at White House parties. After ongoing disputes over trade with France and Britain, President Madison declared war in 1812. The United States, only recently independent, was unprepared for war. On August 24, 1814, Dolley and members of her staff were alerted that British troops were invading Washington, D.C. The Madisons prepared to flee but before they left, Dolley insisted on saving a portrait of George Washington. Today, that painting hangs in the East Room of the White House.

That night, British troops set the White House on fire. The flames destroyed the inside of the house, although most of the exterior walls remained standing. James Hoban, the architect who had designed the house, stepped in once more to oversee the reconstruction. After the president's house was burned, many Americans were outraged, and they united in a renewed sense of patriotism.

First Lady Dolley Madison saved a number of important documents and a painting of George Washington before the White House was set on fire by British troops in 1814.

1801	The President's House is opened to the public on January 1. Thomas Jefferson becomes the new president.
1803	The Louisiana Purchase Treaty is signed.
1809	James Madison becomes president.
1812	The United States declares war on Britain and France.
1814	Britain invades Washington, D.C., and sets fire to the White House. The Madisons salvage some things, including a portrait of George Washington.

11

One of President Abraham Lincoln's was most famous achievements was issuing the Emancipation Proclamation in 1863.

An End to Slavery

Republican president Abraham Lincoln was the fifteenth president to live at the White House. Six weeks after he became president, the United States Civil War began. The northern states (or the Union) fought against the southern states (known as the Confederacy). One major issue was slavery—the northern states believed that slaves should be freed while the southern states disagreed. Perhaps even more important to those in the Union was the idea that the union of states that the country had worked so hard to build was threatened, thus weakening the strength of the nation. In 1861, as the outbreak of war became imminent, Lincoln turned the East Room of the White House into temporary barracks for soldiers about to join the cause.

Lincoln believed there should be an end to slavery, and in 1863, his Emancipation Proclamation was published, which declared that all slaves in the southern states were free. The war lasted from 1861 until 1865, when the Union triumphed, and slavery was finally abolished. In 1865,

When Theodore Roosevelt invited the African American educator Booker T. Washington to have dinner at the White House, the public was outraged.

Time Line				
1823	The Monroe Doctrine is issued, instructing Europe not to colonize the Americas.	1865	President Lincoln is assassinated.
1861	Abraham Lincoln becomes president. With the Civil War about to erupt, soldiers are housed in the White House's East Room.	1874	King David Kalakaua of the Sandwich Islands (Hawaii) is the first ruling monarch to visit the White House.
1863	President Lincoln issues the Emancipation Proclamation.	1877	The first telephone is installed for President Rutherford B. Hayes.

Lincoln was assassinated by John Wilkes Booth, who believed he was helping the Confederate cause. Lincoln's body was placed in a casket in the East Room before his funeral.

No Stranger to Controversy

When President Theodore Roosevelt and his large family moved into the White House in 1901, the building was bursting at the seams. He moved his family to a home on Lafayette Square, in Washington, while architects, engineers, and construction workers built a new wing on the west side of the White House. The wing would house the office of future presidents, cabinet members, and staff, as well as the press room—thus making more room elsewhere for the president's family to live. The youngest president to date, Roosevelt was a modern-minded president who introduced a more assertive foreign policy and other progressive reforms. He was also sometimes controversial, such as when he

President Woodrow Wilson and First Lady Edith Bolling Wilson are pictured here on Armistice Day in 1918.

invited African American educator Booker T. Washington to a White House dinner. Roosevelt thought Washington was an impressive man who would be an interesting guest. Even forty years after the end of slavery, most white Americans at the time held deeply racist views and were offended by this public recognition of a black man.

The Burden of War

Woodrow Wilson became president in 1913. Like Roosevelt before him, Wilson was another passionate believer in democracy. He was reelected for a second term, partly because of his campaign slogan: "He kept us out of war"—as World War I had been underway for three years without any involvement from the United States. However, in 1917, Wilson concluded that he could no longer, in good conscience, hold that stance. After three American ships were sunk by German U-boats (submarines) in the North Atlantic, Wilson requested permission from Congress to declare war on Germany. It was the support that the United States gave to the Allies (Britain, France, Russia, and Italy) that brought Germany to eventual defeat in 1918.

1901	The President's House is officially renamed the "White House" by President Theodore Roosevelt.
1902	The White House undergoes its first major renovation and expansion to make room for the large Roosevelt family.
1909	The Oval Office and Cabinet Room are added to the West Wing.
1913	The first press conference to take place at the White House is given by President Woodrow Wilson.

The White House

President Wilson gave the first-ever press conference from the White House in 1914. Wilson declared that from then on the president would give, ". . . full and free discussion of all large questions of the moment."

Loyalty and Optimism

When Franklin D. Roosevelt became president in 1933, the country was in the middle of the Great Depression, during which 13 million people were unemployed. Roosevelt worked to introduce recovery programs.

President Franklin D. Roosevelt met British Prime Minister Winston Churchill for a meeting aboard a battleship, which resulted in the Anglo-American alliance during World War II.

On December 24, 1929—during Herbert Hoover's presidency—fire had destroyed the West Wing of the White House. Roosevelt took this opportunity to have the Oval Office moved from the center of the building to the southeast corner. This was so that the office could have windows and so the president could get to the West Wing in privacy. Interestingly, the White House was one of the first public buildings in the United States to be equipped with access for people with disabilities—due to the president's use of a wheelchair after suffering from polio.

When war broke out once more in Europe, Roosevelt offered complete assistance to Britain and the Allies but stopped short of sending troops to the front. However, when Japan attacked the U.S. naval base at Pearl Harbor, Hawaii, in December 1941, Roosevelt declared war on Japan and Germany. In 1942, during Roosevelt's administration, an East Wing was added to

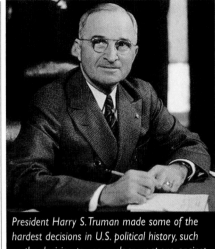

President Harry S. Truman made some of the hardest decisions in U.S. political history, such as the decision to use nuclear weapons against Japan in order to end World War II.

the White House. Today, the wing houses the offices of the First Lady and the Emergency Operations Center which is located in a bunker beneath the East Wing.

Truman Period

After the death of Roosevelt while in office, the next president was Harry S. Truman, who was thrust into one of the most trying times in U.S. presidential history when he took office in 1945. Shortly after becoming president, Truman made the

Time Line		
1914–1918	World War I takes place.	
1929	Fire destroys the West Wing of the White House.	
1933	President Franklin D. Roosevelt gives first his "fireside chat" radio broadcast.	
1939	World War II begins.	
1941	Japan attacks Pearl Harbor.	
1942	East Wing added to White House.	
1945	President Roosevelt dies while in office. President Truman ends World War II by dropping atomic bombs on the Japanese cities of Hiroshima and Nagasaki.	
1950	Three-year structural renovation of White House begins. President Truman orders signing of the United Nations Charter and sets up NATO.	

decision to try to end the war by dropping atomic bombs on the Japanese cities of Hiroshima and Nagasaki. Japan soon surrendered after the devastation these weapons caused. In June 1945, Harry Truman ordered the signing of the Charter of the United Nations. He also set up a military organization called the North Atlantic Treaty Organization, or NATO, to protect Western nations from the perceived communist threat. In 1950, Truman committed U.S. troops to another war, aiding South Korea in fighting against communist North Korea.

Like his leadership decisions, President Truman's ideas for improving the White House also met with controversy. By the middle of the 20th century, the White House was so structurally weak that one of the legs of a piano owned by President Truman's daughter Margaret fell through her bedroom floor to the ceiling of the family dining room below.

John F. Kennedy and his wife, Jacqueline, made an enormous impact during their period in the White House. Jacqueline made radical changes to the mansion's decor.

Despite historians' apprehensions, between 1948 and 1952 the White House underwent the most major renovation it had ever had. At Truman's request, a balcony was built on the south front of the White House. This decision was controversial because many thought it ruined Hoban's original design.

A Promising Career Cut Short

The young and dashing John F. Kennedy took up office in 1961, and the White House changed greatly during his presidency. His wife, Jacqueline, was considered to be among the most elegant of all of the first ladies. Even before she moved into the White House, Mrs. Kennedy began to research ideas about how to redecorate it. At the time, many of the White House's furnishings were reproductions of American antiques, and she was determined to replace them with original American antiques. People from all over the United States donated furniture to her cause. By 1962, the White House had been completely revamped. With popular American television newscaster Walter Cronkite, Mrs. Kennedy unveiled the newly furnished White House in a television program broadcast to the American public.

1962	First Lady Jacqueline Kennedy completely redecorates the interior of the White House.
1963	President John F. Kennedy is assassinated.
1964	President Lyndon Johnson signs the Civil Rights Act in the East Room. Lady Bird Johnson dedicates the East Garden to Jacqueline Kennedy.

Richard Nixon hugs his daughter Julie upon making the decision that he will resign as president of the United States.

President Kennedy had to face a potentially dangerous crisis in October 1962, when American spy planes discovered that Soviet nuclear missiles were set up in Cuba and aimed at the United States. After much negotiation, Kennedy and his advisers were able to settle the crisis with the Soviet Union, which removed the missiles. Kennedy's potential as a great leader was cut short on November 22, 1963, when he was assassinated by Lee Harvey Oswald in Dallas, Texas. Kennedy's body was taken back to Washington, D.C., and his casket was placed in the White House rotunda until his funeral.

An Unsettling Time

Six years after Kennedy's death, Richard M. Nixon became president of the United States. Nixon's years were marred by the ongoing and unpopular Vietnam War and the Watergate scandal. This scandal involved employees of Nixon's Republican reelection committee breaking into Democratic headquarters at the Watergate Hotel in Washington, D.C., and attempting to wiretap the phones in their opponents' offices. After a lengthy trial, several Republican leaders were convicted and others resigned.

Although Nixon ended the Vietnam War in 1973, the Watergate scandal caused him to resign in 1974, the first president in United States history to do so.

The former movie star Ronald Reagan became president in 1981 and held the post until 1989. Though he referred to the Soviet Union as the "evil empire" at the start of his presidency, perhaps the most notable achievement of Reagan's presidency was the improving of relations between the two superpowers. In addition to moving toward peace with the Soviet Union, Reagan also concentrated on cutting taxes at home in the United States. Reagan's vice president, George H. W. Bush, became president in

Charismatic president Bill Clinton's term in office was marred by a personal scandal.

Time Line

1968	Black Civil Rights activist Martin Luther King Jr. and Senator Robert F. Kennedy are assassinated.
1973	U.S. troops withdraw from Vietnam, ending the war.
1974	Richard M. Nixon becomes the first U.S. president to resign from office.
1981	President Ronald Reagan survives an assassination attempt.
1990	The Gulf War begins.
1991	A U.S.-led coalition launches air strikes on Iraq. Persian Gulf War takes place. Iraq is defeated.
1992	U.S. president George W. Bush and Russian president Boris Yeltsin issue a joint statement declaring that their countries no longer "regard each other as potential adversaries."

1989. Perhaps the most notable event of his presidency was the Persian Gulf War, which took place after Iraq invaded Kuwait in the Middle East. When Iraqi troops seemed poised to invade the oil-rich Kuwait, the United Nations ordered Iraq's dictator, Saddam Hussein, to pull back his troops. He ignored the warnings, and in 1991, a coalition of nations organized by President Bush attacked Iraq. The coalition drove the Iraqis out of Kuwait but left Hussein in power.

During the presidency of Bill Clinton, which lasted from 1993 to 2001, the United States enjoyed a strong economy and a time of peace. However, because of his involvement in a personal scandal, Clinton was impeached by the House of Representatives, meaning that the House accused him of having committed, in the words of the Constitution, ". . . high crimes and misdemeanors" that brought his presidency into disrepute. The Senate, the other division of the United States

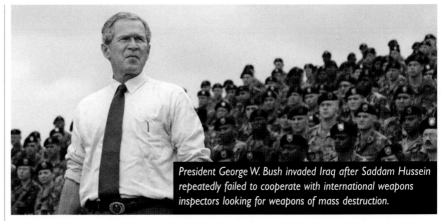

President George W. Bush invaded Iraq after Saddam Hussein repeatedly failed to cooperate with international weapons inspectors looking for weapons of mass destruction.

Congress, however, acquitted Clinton of the charges, and he continued as president. In 1998, Clinton ordered the bombing of Iraq when Saddam Hussein would not cooperate with UN inspectors. They were charged with examining warehouses in Iraq for evidence of illegal weapons.

Terrorist Threat

Eight years after President Bush left office, one of his sons, George W. Bush, became president. During his first year as president, the United States was the victim of a violent act of terrorism when, on September 11, 2001, terrorists from a group called al Qaeda hijacked airplanes and crashed them into the twin towers of the World Trade Center, in New York City, and the Pentagon, in Washington, D.C. The White House was likely to have been the target of a fourth plane that crashed into a field in Pennsylvania after passengers overcame the hijackers. The Bush administration took action against al Qaeda, sending troops to Afghanistan to destroy its bases and topple the Taliban, the government that sheltered it. Not long after that war was won, Bush decided to invade Iraq in order to topple Saddam Hussein. The invasion of Iraq was controversial in the United States as well as around the world. While the Bush administration claimed that that Iraq had weapons of mass destruction that could be given to terrorists, many people believed that George W. Bush was simply trying to finish what his father started in 1991.

1993	The World Trade Center is bombed, suffers minimal damage; 6 people die.
1998	Bill Clinton is charged with lying in court and faces impeachment.
2001	An Islamic militant group called al Qaeda destroys the World Trade Center in New York and damages the Pentagon in Washington. President Bush sends troops into Afghanistan.
2003	Saddam Hussein is captured by U.S. troops and imprisoned in Iraq.

CHAPTER 3

Exploring the White House

The White House, which is located between Pennsylvania Avenue and Constitution Avenue in Washington, D.C., is so much more than the center of the American presidency. It is a living treasure trove of history, art, furnishings, and memories. Echoes of past presidents and their families remain—visible in the portrait galleries and personal touches that linger from the various terms of office through the past two hundred years. The White House still serves as the home of the current president and his family. And what a magnificent home it is!

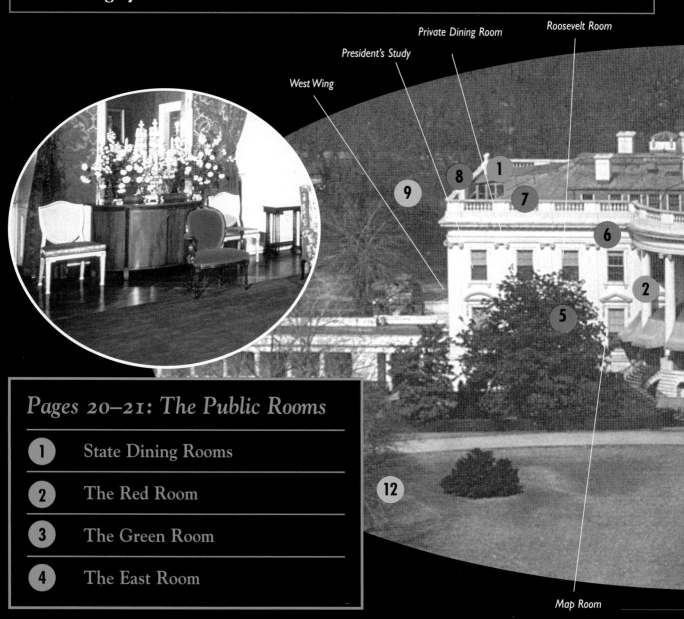

West Wing

President's Study

Private Dining Room

Roosevelt Room

Map Room

Pages 20–21: The Public Rooms

1. State Dining Rooms

2. The Red Room

3. The Green Room

4. The East Room

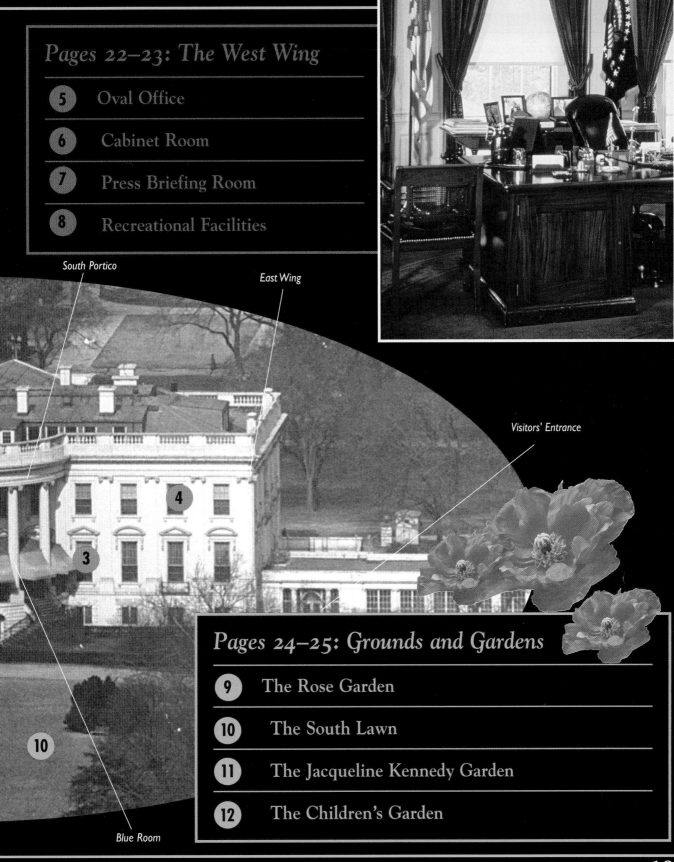

South Portico

East Wing

Visitors' Entrance

4

3

10

Blue Room

① State Dining Room

The State Dining Room can seat as many as 140 guests. The magnificent gilded bronze centerpiece bought by President Monroe often graces the table. The room was enlarged when President Theodore Roosevelt had the West Wing built in 1902. To accommodate more guests, the long mahogany table is often replaced by smaller tables.

The room at the southwest corner of the Public Rooms is the State Dining Room. Notable pieces of silverware and glassware chosen by different presidents grace the large mahogany table.

The Red Room has served many different purposes over the years. Theodore Roosevelt's children used it as a playroom.

② The Red Room

The Red Room is furnished in the Empire Style of the early 19th century and is currently used as a reception room. First Lady Jackie Kennedy styled the room, and her decor has been maintained over the years. In 1902, the walls were covered with red satin fabric with a gold design on the border. The carpet is beige, red, and gold. Over the fireplace hangs a portrait of President Martin Van Buren's daughter-in-law, Angelica Singleton Van Buren, who served as his First Lady. First Lady Eleanor Roosevelt used to hold press conferences for female reporters in the Red Room.

③ The Green Room

Thomas Jefferson used the Green Room as a dining room, but today it is a small parlor that is a good place for quiet conversation. It has been the site of small gatherings and televised interviews. The walls are covered in green silk, and the furniture is from the earliest years of the White House, although none of it is original to the mansion. Among the paintings in the Green Room is a New Jersey beach scene by Henry Tanner, the first African American to have work displayed in the White House.

The Green Room was used as a dining room by Thomas Jefferson and as a card room by James Monroe.

The East Room is sparsely decorated. Its Steinway piano and large open floor make it a good choice for music recitals.

④ The East Room

The East Room is the largest room in the White House, and it has served many functions, including being used as a movie theater. When he designed the White House, James Hoban intended the East Room as a public-audience room. The room contains three chandeliers, each of which has more than 6,000 pieces of glass. The painting of George Washington by Gilbert Stuart, saved by Dolley Madison in 1814, hangs in the East Room. This painting is the only item in the White House that has remained there since 1800.

5 Oval Office

The president's office, otherwise known as the Oval Office, is the best-known room in the West Wing. Each president or first lady

The famous Oval Office has its shape so that many of the president's advisors can gather around his desk at one time.

designs a rug with the presidential seal for the office. The president can select which paintings he wants to hang on the walls. George W. Bush, for example, chose several paintings of his home state of Texas, along with portraits of Abraham Lincoln and George Washington. John F. Kennedy, on the other hand, decorated the walls with naval paintings and watercolors. Jacqueline Kennedy chose red carpet for the office and, ironically, it was being installed at the very moment that her husband was assassinated.

6 Cabinet Room

Many serious meetings take place in the Cabinet Room, where members of the president's cabinet, the National Security Council, Congress, and heads of state meet to discuss national and world issues. The room holds an oval mahogany table and leather chairs, and each member of the president's cabinet is assigned a seat according to when his or her department was established.

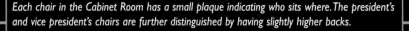

Each chair in the Cabinet Room has a small plaque indicating who sits where. The president's and vice president's chairs are further distinguished by having slightly higher backs.

7 Press Briefing Room

The Press Briefing Room was built above the pool President Franklin Roosevelt used. In 2000, 18 miles (29 km) of cable were laid under the floor to accommodate technological needs. Every day, members of the press come to the room to learn the latest news from the White House. At the front of the room is a podium in front of blue draperies and the seal of the White House. Usually, the White House press secretary conducts press briefings. The journalists who gather daily for the briefing are called the White House press corps.

President Clinton delivers a speech before the distinctive seal and curtain of the Press Briefing Room.

8 Recreational Facilities

Because Franklin D. Roosevelt's pool was turned into the Press Briefing Room, President Gerald Ford had another swimming pool built in the White House in 1975. Other recreational facilities in the White House include a bowling alley, a tennis court, a jogging track, a movie theater, a practice putting green, and a billiard room.

Every president needs some time off. In this picture, President Nixon is shown stepping over the foul line as he delivers his ball down one of the White House's bowling lanes.

The Rose Garden is situated just outside the West Wing. It contains many different breeds of roses. Occasionally, the president will deliver a public address from the Rose Garden, as President Reagan is shown doing here in 1986.

9 The Rose Garden

The Rose Garden, otherwise known as the West Garden, is perhaps the best-known area on White House grounds. The garden was created by First Lady Ellen Wilson, Woodrow Wilson's first wife, in 1913. During the Kennedy administration, the garden was redesigned so it could be used for outdoor ceremonies. Besides roses, the garden has several types of tulips, grape hyacinth, lavender cotton, and crab-apple trees. Occasionally, the president will give speeches, hold ceremonies, or make announcements in the Rose Garden.

10 The South Lawn

The large expanse of grass on the south side of the White House is called the South Lawn. Sometimes, elaborate marquees are set up on the lawn for parties and concerts. The South Lawn is also the site of the annual Easter Egg Roll.

Many past presidents and first ladies have planted trees and shrubs on the South Lawn.

The East Garden was dedicated by Lady Bird Johnson to Jacqueline Kennedy in 1965.

11 The Jacqueline Kennedy Garden

Like the Rose Garden, the Jacqueline Kennedy Garden is based on traditional 18th-century American garden design. The idea for the garden came from the Kennedys, and after President Kennedy's assassination, Lady Bird Johnson completed the plan and dedicated the garden to Mrs. Kennedy. The garden is framed by a holly hedge and planted with holly trees, tulips, pansies, and grape hyacinth. It also includes an herb garden that is used by White House chefs.

12 The Children's Garden

President and Mrs. Lyndon B. Johnson presented the Children's Garden garden to the White House. It has a goldfish pond, an apple tree, and a paved area that features footprints and handprints of past presidents' children and grandchildren.

The Children's Garden was President and Mrs. Johnson's idea for capturing memories of presidents' children through the years.

CHAPTER 4

The People

The White House has seen many people come and go since it was first occupied by President John Adams in 1800. More than forty presidents have called the White House home since then, arguably spending the most important years of their lives there. Besides the presidents, there have been the many first ladies and children living in the White House. And, of course, the first families had to bring their pets with them to their new home.

An Independent Man

Thomas Jefferson became president in 1801, at which time he was already connected to the White House. Not only was he secretary of state under George Washington, but he participated in the contest held to select a design for the building and even submitted his own plan. While Jefferson is known to have disliked the grandness of the White House, some think he added to it by hiring workers to install more carved garlands, wreaths, and other decorations above doors and around windows. Jefferson oversaw perhaps the greatest land purchase the United States ever made when, in 1803, Napoleon agreed to sell Louisiana—which comprised much of what is now the central United States—to help fund his war in Europe. Soon after the purchase, Jefferson sent Meriwether Lewis and William Clark on an expedition to discover what lay west of the Mississippi. As they traveled, they sent back artifacts, including animal pelts, Native American objects, plant specimens, and animal bones. Jefferson displayed these in the entrance hall of the White House, which was open to public view.

The Madisons

The next president was James Madison. He was a popular politician and played a large role in the development of the United

The four presidents whose faces are carved into Mout Rushmore – George Washington, Thomas Jefferson, Theodore Roosevelt and Abraham Lincoln – represent the first 150 years of the U.S. presidency.

Tales & Customs — Children's Parties

President Andrew Jackson, who served from 1865 to 1869, sometimes hosted children's parties at the White House. One White House staffer, Colonel William H. Crook, wrote about one of them: "There has never been a children's party so wonderful . . . The dancing was in the East Room. There were a great many square dances, and a few waltzes and polkas; but the fancy dances were the best . . . ."

Thomas Jefferson is best remembered for drafting the Declaration of Independence.

States Constitution. His wife Dolley was also well-liked and regarded as an excellent hostess.

In fact, she was a popular guest at White House functions well after her husband's death. Because the State Dining Room was so cold, the Madisons had a furnace installed in the White House basement.

The Huge Cheese

While Andrew Jackson, the seventh president, is known for his war heroism, perhaps one of the more infamous incidents that occurred during his presidency concerned a giant wheel of cheese. Weighing more than 1,400 pounds (635 kilograms), the giant wheel of cheddar was a gift from a Jackson supporter in New York. The cheese sat in the White House entrance hall for more than two years. In the weeks before Jackson left office, he invited the public to come and have a taste. It took only two hours for the cheese to be devoured. However, White House staff claimed that it took several years for the odor from the cheese to go away and for the stain it left on the floor to be removed.

A statue of President Andrew Johnson stands near the White House in Washington, D.C.

The White House

Soldiers in the East Room

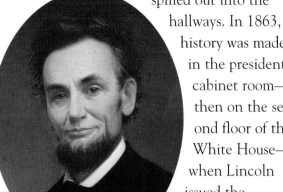
Abraham Lincoln endured a great deal of grief during his time in office.

Abraham Lincoln is one of the most well-known and loved of the United States presidents. He endured much sadness during his four years in the White House. Besides the tragic death of his middle son, Willie, Lincoln watched the nation he loved split apart by the political differences of the Civil War, which took place during most of his presidency. When Lincoln called for troops to sign up to fight for the Union in 1861, thousands of men came to Washington in response. They quickly filled up hotels and boarding houses and, eventually, came to the White House. Soldiers from Kansas slept in the East Room, and more troops spilled out into the hallways. In 1863, history was made in the president's cabinet room—then on the second floor of the White House—when Lincoln issued the Emancipation Proclamation, declaring about four million slaves to be free.

Fireside Chats

Theodore Roosevelt's fifth cousin, Franklin D. Roosevelt, was president for twelve years and lived in the White House longer than any other president. From the White House, Roosevelt conducted regular "fireside chats" that were broadcast on the radio. The chats were popular with the American public, giving them the feeling that the president was accessible and

President Franklin D. Roosevelt delivered regular broadcasts to the American people.

Tales & Customs — Who Pays?

The general impression projected to the public is that the president and his family live like royalty in the White House. However, this is not strictly true. When food is purchased for an official White House function, the U.S. government pays. But when the president, first lady, or their children want a personal meal or snack, they are charged for it. Few Americans realize that part of the president's salary goes towards the cost of food.

28

American children often learn the names of White House pets. The spaniel Rex is shown here with his owners, President Ronald and First Lady Nancy Reagan.

that he wanted to come into their living rooms to talk with them. Roosevelt's wife, Eleanor, surprised the press and the public by holding press conferences for women reporters, who were not allowed to attend presidential press conferences. The conferences were usually held in the Red Room, and sometimes Mrs. Roosevelt would knit as she talked. Eleanor Roosevelt was an important first lady who became involved in many social and humanitarian programs.

Mischief-making

Often, by the time the president and first lady came to the White House, their children were grown up and living away from home. But some presidents had young children who lived with them in the White House. President Abraham Lincoln's sons, Willie and Tad, were only eleven and eight when their father became president. They had great fun in the White House. For example, they would ring the servants' bells in differ-

ent parts of the house to confuse the servants about where to go next. After his son Willie died, President Lincoln bought Tad two goats, Nanny and Nanko, that Tad liked to bring inside the house and chase up and down the hallways. The Lincolns had other pets as well, including a turkey that President Lincoln had planned to kill and eat for Thanksgiving dinner. However, when the time came, Tad pleaded with his father to spare the turkey's life. The president agreed, and the Lincoln White House had another pet.

The Lincoln years were not the only time there were goats in the White House. Benjamin Harrison's grandchildren kept a pet goat named His Whiskers.

They hooked His Whiskers up to a cart, and the goat pulled them around the White House grounds.

The Roosevelt Clan

Perhaps the most memorable presidential family was that of Theodore Roosevelt. Along with his wife, Edith, he had six children. The Roosevelt children filled the White House with happy noise, sometimes even chaos. They took metal trays from the kitchen and used them to slide down staircases, and they roller-skated down corridors throughout the mansion. One rainy afternoon, Quentin Roosevelt had two friends over to play, and they thought it would be fun to throw spitballs at the portraits of presidents hanging in the White House. When President Roosevelt saw the spitballs on the paintings, he ordered Quentin and his friends to clean off every last one and then decided Quentin could have no friends over to play until the president decided his punishment had lasted long enough. Quentin created more commotion when he took his pony, Algonquin, up to the second floor in the White House elevator to cheer up his sick brother, Archie. To add to the hilarity in the White House, the Roosevelt clan had many other pets, including a lizard, guinea pigs, a pig, a badger, a hyena, a macaw, and a rooster.

President Carter's daughter Amy is shown here sitting in the tree house her father designed for her on the White House grounds.

Entertaining the Kids

In 1977, Jimmy Carter became president. His daughter Amy was nine years old at the time and the youngest of the Carter children. For the most part, she was the only child in the White House, so she had to find ways to amuse herself. President Carter designed a tree house for Amy in 1977. It was built on a platform on stilts among the trees on the South Lawn. When the Carters left the White House in 1981, the tree house was taken apart and put in White House storage, where it is kept as a historic object. Another daughter of a recent president, Chelsea Clinton, had a cat named Socks, and her father, Bill Clinton, was often seen with his chocolate Labrador retriever, Buddy.

Theodore Roosevelt's son Quentin is remembered for mischief-making at the White House. He once took his pony up to the second floor to visit his sick brother.

Tales & Customs — Supreme Service

First Lady Nancy Reagan wrote in her book, My Turn: *"Every evening while I took a bath, one of the maids would come by and remove my clothes for laundering or dry cleaning. The bed would always be turned down. Five minutes after Ronnie [President Ronald Reagan] came home and hung up his suit, it would disappear from the closet to be pressed, cleaned, or brushed. No wonder Ron used to call the White House an eight-star hotel."*

White Weddings

The White House has been the site of many joyous occasions throughout its history. Perhaps the most notable of these are the seventeen weddings that have taken place there. The first wedding in the White House was in 1812, when Dolley Madison's sister, Lucy Payne Washington—the widow of George Washington's nephew—married Supreme Court Justice Thomas Todd. Only one president has been married in the White House—

Grover Cleveland, who married Frances Folsom in 1886. Frances was twenty-seven years younger than President Cleveland—and at twenty-one years old, the youngest first lady ever.

The wedding took place in the flower-filled Blue Room, and famous bandleader John Philips Sousa led the band in the "Wedding March." Esther, the Cleveland's second daughter, is the only president's child who was born in the White House.

President Grover Cleveland and Frances Folsom married at the White House in 1886. Cleveland is the only president to marry there while in office.

31

The White House

Richard Nixon's daughter, Tricia, is one of a few presidents' children who got married at the White House during their father's presidency.

Presidents' Daughters

The daughters of several presidents have been married in the White House. The first was James Monroe's daughter Maria, whose wedding ceremony took place in 1820. In 1874, the wedding of Nellie Grant, daughter of President Ulysses S. Grant, to Algernon Sartoris took place in the East Room, with a wedding breakfast following in the State Dining Room. One wedding ceremony that fascinated the press—and the entire nation—was that of Alice Roosevelt, daughter of President Theodore Roosevelt. Nicknamed "Princess Alice" by the press, the president's daughter had already captured the attention of the country with her free-spirited and fun-loving nature. Her 1906 wedding to Ohio congressman Nicholas Longworth received attention from around the world. The ceremony took place in the East Room, and the reception was in the State Dining Room. Other presidents' daughters who have been married in the White House include Tricia Nixon, who, in 1971, married Edward Cox in the first White House Ceremony to be held in the Rose Garden.

Sadness and Sorrow

The White House has also been the scene of great sorrow. Perhaps the most touching

episode occurred on February 20, 1862, when President Lincoln's son Willie died of typhoid fever. His parents were devastated by his death, but Mrs. Lincoln, in particular, never really recovered. Willie's body was displayed in the Green Room, as far away

Tales & Customs — Deaths in the White House

Only two presidents have died inside the White House. They are William Henry Harrison, who died of pneumonia in 1841, and Zachary Taylor, who died in 1850 after suffering a bout of gastroenteritis. Several first ladies have died in the White House, including Letitia Tyler, in 1842; Caroline Scott Harrison, in 1892; and Ellen Wilson, in 1914.

The procession bearing President John F. Kennedy's casket departed from the White House on November 25, 1963. Kennedy's untimely death was caused by an assassin's bullet.

Underneath the White House are underground bunkers to be used during times of national emergency, and on that day, Cheney was rushed to one of these bunkers to ensure that he would be safe in case the White House or other government buildings were attacked. This bunker is called the PEOC—short for "Presidential Emergency Operations Center." It is fully equipped with the latest communications technology. Later, it was discovered that the White House was a likely target for the plane that crashed in a field in Pennsylvania on September 11.

from his mother's room as possible, and his funeral was held in the East Room. Three years later, Abraham Lincoln's body was also displayed in the East Room. The victim of an assassin's bullet, Lincoln died on April 14, 1865.

Almost one hundred years later, the body of another assassinated president lay in state in the East Room. John F. Kennedy had been visiting Dallas, Texas, on November 22, 1963, when he was shot and killed by Lee Harvey Oswald. Kennedy's body was flown to Washington, D.C., and his flag-draped casket was displayed in the East Room on the same catafalque that had held Lincoln's body in 1865.

A Day of Terror

George W. Bush was president on September 11, 2001, when terrorists attacked the World Trade Center towers in New York City and the Pentagon in Washington, D.C. Bush was visiting a school in Florida at the time, but Vice President Dick Cheney was at the White House.

The sight of the burning twin towers of the World Trade Center sent a wave of shock across the Western world.

CHAPTER 5

Significant Events

The White House has played host to hundreds of special guests, including dignitaries, heads of state, presidents, and royal figures from around the world. Whatever the reasons for their visits, these distinguished visitors were always given a comfortable and memorable stay, courtesy of White House staff. Countless concerts, recitals, and performances in the styles favored by the sitting presidents have taken place at the White House.

First Lady Nancy Reagan made a point of sampling all dishes before they were served to any distinguished White House guests.

Planning

A great deal of planning goes into each state and official visit to the White House. Months before the visit is to occur, White House staff begin working out the details. They do research to find out what kinds of food the visiting dignitaries like, what colors of flowers they prefer, and what kind of music they enjoy.

They must also make sure that nothing would offend visitors for religious or other reasons. For example, in China the color white symbolizes death and mourning, so white flowers would be avoided when guests from China are visiting. In the days leading up to the event, a detailed schedule of everything that is to occur during the visit is written and studied to make sure that nothing is left to chance. The White House Social Office even keeps extra hair dryers, hosiery, shoes, and dresses in case a guest has an emergency need.

The head chef comes up with many ideas for dishes to serve for the occasion, and staff members, the first lady, and sometimes even the president all sample the food and provide opinions. On the days before the state visit, staff members study the White House to make sure

President Ford waltzed with Queen Elizabeth II at a State Dinner celebrating the American Bicentennial in 1976.

White House visits are divided into three categories. State visits are reserved for heads of state, such as kings, queens, and presidents. Official visits are for prime ministers or other heads of government. The third category is "working visits," which includes meetings with the president and his cabinet or with other members of government. State visits and official visits require arrival ceremonies and state dinners.

everything is in order, checking to make sure the walls are cleanly painted and there are no scuff marks on the floors.

Notable Visitors

Among the notable visitors have been King David Kalakua of the Sandwich Islands—now the state of Hawaii—who in 1874 was the first monarch to attend a state dinner. During World War II, many dignitaries visited with President Franklin D. Roosevelt to discuss the war, including King George and Queen Elizabeth of Great Britain, British prime minister Winston Churchill, the king of Greece, the queen of Holland, and Madame Chiang Kai-Shek of China. The first pope to visit the White House was John Paul II, who arrived in 1979 during Jimmy Carter's presidency. Recent historic events at the White House include the signing of a peace treaty by Egyptian president Anwar Sadat and

Pope John Paul II and President Jimmy Carter shared a lighter moment during a reception on the North Lawn in 1979.

Israeli prime minister Menachem Begin in 1978, also during the Carter administration. In the East Room in 1987, President Ronald Reagan and Soviet President Mikhail Gorbachev signed the world's first arms control agreement, called the Intermediate Nuclear Force Treaty. In 1993, President Clinton and 3,000 guests watched as Prime Minister Yitzhak Rabin of Israel and Palestine Liberation Organization Chairman Yasser Arafat, signed a historic agreement on the South Lawn.

The White House

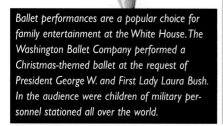

Ballet performances are a popular choice for family entertainment at the White House. The Washington Ballet Company performed a Christmas-themed ballet at the request of President George W. and First Lady Laura Bush. In the audience were children of military personnel stationed all over the world.

Cultural Events

The White House has been the site of numerous concerts and other cultural events. The first reception at the White House was held in 1801, and the United States Marine Band played. Ever since, the band has made regular visits to the White House, and it is even called "The President's Own." During President Lincoln's administration, he had the band perform concerts on the White House grounds every week.

The Kennedy administration is remembered for the many important cultural events held in the White House during its time. Groups such as the Jerome Robbins Ballet, Metropolitan Opera Studio, and the American Shakespeare Festival performed at the White House, as did distinguished performers such as composer and conductor

Leonard Bernstein and Pablo Casals. The Casals concert was considered noteworthy because Casals had first played at the White House in 1904 but after 1938 refused to visit the United States because he disagreed with its policies toward his native

Tales & Customs — Athletes at the White House

Athletes and sports teams who have won their sports' highest honors are regularly invited to the White House. In 2003, for example, the winners of baseball's World Series, the Florida Marlins, were congratulated at the White House by President George W. Bush, as were the winners of the National Basketball Championship, the San Antonio Spurs. Individual athletes, such as six-time Tour de France winner Lance Armstrong and various Olympic medal winners, also have been honored at the White House.

In 1798, the U.S. Marine Band, shown here in 1996, was created by President John Adams. The tradition has been maintained ever since, and there are currently 143 musicians in the band.

country, Spain. He agreed to return and perform because he admired President John F. Kennedy. The concert was televised in the United States. Sometimes a guest will mention a favorite performer or even request someone specific. Among the many guests welcomed to the White House by President Bill Clinton and First Lady Hillary Clinton was President Vaclav Havel of the Czech Republic.

Many Musical Styles

When the president and first lady consider whom to ask to entertain at a state dinner, they sometimes have difficulty deciding who would be best, but in the case of the dinner for President Havel, it was easy. He had already told the Clintons about his admiration for American musician Lou Reed, whose music, he said, inspired him as he fought against commu-

nism in his country. The Clintons asked Lou Reed to perform, and he agreed. He was accompanied by Czech bassist Milan Hlavsa. Musicians from other countries also perform at the White House. In 1916, President Woodrow Wilson enjoyed a concert by Australian pianist and composer Percy Grainger. For a visit by British prime minister Tony Blair, the Clintons asked Elton John to sing with American musician Stevie Wonder. Other performers have included Eric Clapton, cellist Yo-Yo Ma, and U2 lead singer Bono.

One event that is held at the end of each year is a reception for recipients of the Kennedy Center Honors. These awards are for Americans who have made significant contributions to the performing arts. Among recent recipients are Bill Cosby, Shirley Temple Black, Jack Nicholson, and Loretta Lynn.

Sir Elton John (second from left) and Stevie Wonder (second from right) were invited to perform together at the White House in honor of British prime minister Tony Blair (far left) in 1998.

The White House

Inaugurations

The ceremony during which the president of the United States takes the oath of office is called the inauguration. Only six presidents have taken the oath in the White House, while others have taken place in other government buildings, such as the United States Capitol, also in Washington, D.C. The first was Rutherford B. Hayes, who took the oath on Saturday, March 3, 1877. Because the usual day for a president's inauguration at the time, March 4, was a Sunday, the ceremony was privately held in the Red Room of the White House. Hayes's public inauguration took place on Monday, March 5. President Franklin D. Roosevelt's fourth and final inauguration took place on the South Portico of the White House on January 20, 1945, possibly because Roosevelt used a wheel-

Franklin D. Roosevelt delivered his inaugural address to a crowd of thousands from the South Portico of the White House on January 20, 1945.

Tales & Customs — "The People Would Rule"

The following was written about Andrew Jackson's inauguration at the White House: "Cut glass and china to the amount of several thousand dollars had been broken in the struggle to get the refreshments . . . . Ladies fainted, men were seen with bloody noses . . . . It is mortifying to see men with boots heavy with mud, standing on the damask-satin-covered chairs and sofas . . . . But it was the People's day, and the People's President, and the People would rule."

chair at the time, something he typically kept a secret from the American public. Roosevelt died that April, and his vice president, Harry S. Truman, took the oath of office in the Cabinet Room of the West Wing of the White House almost immediately.

The inauguration of Dwight D. Eisenhower took place privately in the White House in 1957 in the East Room. When Richard Nixon resigned in August 1974, Vice President Gerald Ford took the oath of office in the East Room and became president. Ronald Reagan was sworn in on January 20, 1985. Because it was a Sunday, he was sworn in privately in the North Entrance Hall. He was sworn in publicly the next day.

The Jackson Inaugural Reception

James and Dolley Madison began the tradition of holding inaugu-

President Dwight Eisenhower and his wife, Mamie, responded to a cheering crowd during his inauguration in 1953.

ral receptions and balls at the White House. But after Lincoln's presidency, the crowds became too large for the White House to accommodate. Perhaps the most memorable example of this problem occurred at the inaugural reception of Andrew Jackson in 1829. Jackson wanted to be thought of as a man of the people, so he invited the public to the White House for refreshments and drinks after his inauguration. White House staff were shocked when huge mobs of people rushed into the White House, ate all the food, and broke dishes and glasses. Women fainted, men with muddy boots stood on White House furniture to get a better look at the president, and fights broke out as people argued over who would get the last drink or slice of cake. Finally, members of Jackson's staff formed a chain to keep the crowd away from the president, and he escaped out a back door.

CHAPTER 6

A Day in the Life

The activities of each day at the White House depend on what the president and first lady have scheduled and what is going on in the world. Some White House events, however, are fairly predictable. Staff members show up to do their jobs, some arriving as early as 7 A.M. There is always food to prepare, floors to be cleaned, and phones and mail to be answered. The White House buzzes with activity nearly twenty-four hours a day.

The National Park Services are responsible for keeping the White House grounds immaculate. This includes trimming the White House Christmas tree each year.

Behind the Scenes

It takes a lot of work to keep the White House—with its 132 rooms—clean and in good repair, especially with up to 6,000 tourists and other visitors arriving every day. The person in charge of the ninety full-time staff is called the chief usher.

The White House kitchen employs five chefs plus kitchen staff. The executive chef is carefully selected by the First Lady. The cooking staff, along with all of the White House residence staff, remain when a new president moves into the White House. To prepare for a state dinner, one of the chefs might visit the library to learn more about the foods and customs of the country from which the guest is coming. The staff also makes sure it is aware of any dietary restrictions guests may have.

Other behind-the-scenes staff include the chief floral designer, who is responsible for ensuring that flower arrangements are fresh and watered. Along with other staff florists, he or she creates stunning centerpieces for events held at the White House. Because invitations to White House functions are traditionally handwritten, three calligraphers are on staff to produce the thousands of invitations that are mailed each month. They also handwrite menus and place cards. The exterior walls of the White House and its grounds are part of the National Park Service. The 18 acres (7.2 hectares) that make up the White House complex are carefully tended by gardeners employed by the National Park

Service. Employees are also responsible for putting up the White House Christmas tree and decorating the grounds for the holidays.

The White House is open to the public for tours, except on Sundays and Mondays. Tourists have a choice of taking a self-guided tour, on which they can tour the mansion at their own

The president often takes long flights to meet with other leaders.

Scott McLellan, press secretary to President George W. Bush, answers reporters' questions at a press conference.

pace, or they can take a tour guided by one of their representatives or senators, if they give the congressperson's office at least eight weeks' notice.

Press Briefings

Some other events that occur on a regular basis are press briefings. These are given every day and usually last no more than an hour. Generally, the president's press secretary conducts press briefings. His or her job is to act as a spokesperson for the president and answer each question the way the president would. It is vital for that person to maintain regular contact with the president and his staff. The journalists

who regularly attend these press briefings are called the White House press corps. Some of them have been performing this function for decades.

The President's Work Day

The president spends his days meeting with advisers and attending meetings and functions. He may spend an entire day with members of his cabinet or he may fly to any one of the fifty states on business. Sometimes, the president goes abroad to meet with leaders of other nations. To make sure he can fit everything into a day, the president usually rises early and goes to bed early.

Tales & Customs — The First Lady

The First Lady's responsibilities are many and varied. She helps staff members prepare for White House social functions and acts as hostess at each one. Some First Ladies, such as Eleanor Roosevelt, have been deeply involved in social programs and projects. The role of the First Lady is not clearly defined, and each woman brings her personality and attitude to the role. Most Americans, however, seem to believe that the First Lady's primary responsibility is to support her husband.

Uncovering the Past

The United States president's home is living history. Everything possible has been done to preserve the house itself and the treasures and furnishings that have found their way into it throughout the many presidencies. However, there have been so many renovations, improvements, and additions to the White House —both structural and decorative—that, without the efforts of historians, archaeologists, and engineers, it would be easy to forget the precious details of its various incarnations.

Relic Kits

The only real excavation of the White House was ordered by Harry Truman in 1948. A committee of engineers determined that the mansion was deteriorating. On December 13, 1949, work crews began dismantling the inside of the White House. As they took apart the wooden floors, each floorboard was numbered so it could be replaced exactly where it was.

Many of the scraps from the broken pieces or from materials that were determined to be unnecessary to save were put into "relic kits" and sold to the public. For example, one kit contained a chunk of pine. Another had a chunk of sandstone and a nail. The largest kit provided enough stone or brick to build a fireplace. Money from the sale of the kits helped to pay for the White House's renovation.

During Harry Truman's presidency, the White House underwent its most comprehensive renovation ever. This involved pulling up floorboards and restabilizing the foundations of the building.

Hidden Beneath

As workers removed the interior walls of the White House, they revealed the interior lining that had been used to build the mansion in the 1790s and in the rebuilding after the 1814 fire. They saw that behind the exterior sandstone walls were several layers of brick that were sealed with whitewash. Work crews found a marble box that had been hidden under the Entrance Hall, and inside the box was a bottle of rye whisky. Historians figure the liquor was placed there during Prohibition years—1919 to 1933—when Americans were forbidden to buy alcoholic beverages. Workers also found a brick that had the imprint of a dog's paw. They also found charred timbers and sandstone, evidence of the fire set by the British during the War of 1812. Laborers also saw that the inside

The White House requires regular waterblasting to remove dirt from its exterior. In the 1980s, a thorough cleaning revealed many fine details.

of the exterior walls had ducts used by an old furnace heating system, as well as hand-powered bell systems that at one time were used to summon servants and staff. President Truman, who always enjoyed studying history, followed the demolition closely and was fascinated by the details of the White House in former years. He was particularly interested in seeing the marks left by the Scottish stonemasons, who had used their chisels to carve Masonic symbols into the stone.

Mystery of the Cornerstone

In an attempt to find the cornerstone laid by the Masons in a 1792 ceremony, Truman and architect Lorenzo Winslow searched the walls with a metal detector, which they hoped would locate a brass plaque said to be on the stone. They reported that the loudest buzz from the detector was at the southwest corner, but Truman was against destroying the exterior wall to get to it, so the exact location of the cornerstone is still a mystery.

President Truman ordered a thorough investigation with a metal detector to discover where the White House's original cornerstone is located.

Preserving the Past

Restoration is a constant requirement at the White House. Since Truman ordered the White House's most comprehensive renovation project in the 1950s, many alterations have taken place. During the 1990s, the Committee for Preservation of the White House was revived with the purpose of determining what renovations were required and when. Beginning in this period, restoration projects have included the reupholstering of seventy-three pieces of furniture and pillows, the repairing of two floors, and the hanging of new curtains or drapes in twenty-eight windows.

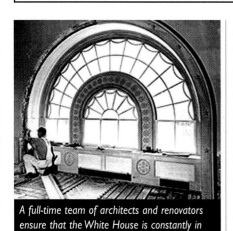

A full-time team of architects and renovators ensure that the White House is constantly in prime condition.

Time and Nature

The restoration was not funded by public funds but by private donations, many of which were from the White House Historical Association. This association was formed in 1961 at the request of the National Park Service and with the encouragement of First Lady Jackie Kennedy. The association raises money by publishing and selling educational materials. In July 1962, among its first publications was *The White House: An Historic Guide.* An updated version of the book continues to be published today, and money from its sales go to preserving the White House. The Clinton-era restoration was also funded by donations from the National Park Service, which maintains the White House and its grounds. Such donations are necessary because the government presently gives each administration only $50,000 per administration to decorate the mansion.

Beginning in 1988, in preparation for the 200th anniversary of the laying of the White House cornerstone in 1992, architects and historians began a close examination of every part of the

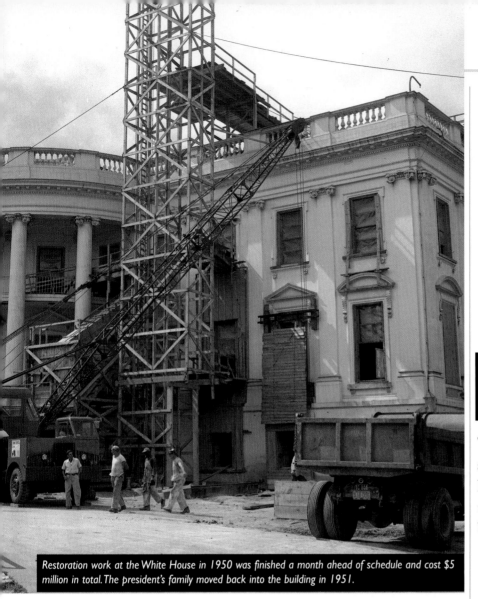

Restoration work at the White House in 1950 was finished a month ahead of schedule and cost $5 million in total. The president's family moved back into the building in 1951.

The restoration of pieces of furniture, such as this chair first purchased by President Monroe, ensures that early pieces from the White House can remain in use.

White House. They took notes and kept records of the sandstone blocks on the exterior of the building and then moved inside and studied each wall, door, window frame, and piece of trim. The more than 850 pages they ended up with will be valuable in future renovation and restoration of the White House.

The White House has been standing for more than two hundred years and is perhaps the best-loved building in the United States. Fortunately, those who have worked so hard to become residents of the White House usually respect its traditions and history. The White House symbolizes so much that makes the United States what it is: a nation of hard work, diversity, and strength.

Tales & Customs — A Sense of Continuity

In 1901, Theodore Roosevelt said: "The White House is the property of the nation, and so far as it is compatible with living therein should be kept as it originally was, for the same reasons that we keep Mount Vernon [George Washington's home] as it originally was. . . . It is a good thing to preserve such buildings as historic monuments, which keep alive our sense of continuity with the nation's past."

Glossary

administration: the group centered around a president in office.

advocate: a person who publicly supports a cause or idea.

al Qaeda: a widespread anti-western terrorist network that gives money, logistical support, and training to a wide variety of radical Islamist terrorist groups.

American Revolution: the war that took place from 1775 to 1783 in which the American colonies won independence from British rule.

Anglo-Palladian: an 18th-century architectural style combining the technique of 16th-century Italian architect Andrea Palladio with English architectural styles.

assassination: the murder of a political, religious, or otherwise well-known figure.

Axis powers: the three countries—Germany, Italy, and Japan—that fought against the Allies in World War II.

barracks: a large building or group of buildings for housing soldiers.

bunker: a heavily fortified underground chamber.

cabinet: a group of senior government officials who act as advisers to a president or prime minister.

catafalque: an ornamental platform on which a coffin is placed during a funeral.

colonnade: a set of regularly spaced columns supporting a roof.

commissioner: a representative with governmental authority.

communism: the political and economic system that aims to create a classless society in which all property is owned by the state, which is controlled by a single, unelected party.

Confederacy: the southern states of the United States that separated from the northern states in 1860–1861. The northern states were known as the Union.

congress: a national law-making body.

controversy: public debate about a matter that arouses strong public opinion.

cornerstone: a stone that forms the base of the corner of a building.

curator: a person who is responsible for caring for a place in which items are exhibited, such as a museum.

Declaration of Independence: the document signed on July 4, 1776, that declared the United States of America to be independent of the British Crown.

decommission: to remove or withdraw from active service.

décor: a decorative style or scheme, such as would be applied to a room.

democracy: the form of government rules with the consent of the people and power is exercised through elected officials.

dignitary: a person who holds a high position or rank.

diplomat: a person who is responsible for conducting negotiations between nations.

dumbwaiter: a small elevator used to transport food or other small items from one floor to another using a pulley system.

emancipation: freedom from legal, social, or political restrictions.